John Berryman died here

Alex Stolis

Cyberwit.net
HIG 45 Kaushambi Kunj, Kalindipuram
Allahabad - 211011 (U.P.) India
http://www.cyberwit.net
Tel: +(91) 9415091004 +(91) (532) 2552257
E-mail: info@cyberwit.net

Printed at Repro India Limited.

Contents

Dream Song 227 [January 7, 1972; no Henry, no Mr. Bones]

and no John fucking Berryman; coward bastard taking a flight
without a real plan. I saw a ghost; or rather will choose to call
it a ghost; it was no apparition, no long lost soul feeling bitter

sweet and lukewarm about the afterlife. I walk barefoot because
I like to feel the need; like to feel the ever so slight quiver in the
floorboards as you practice your morning yoga. You tried to teach

me once: half-moon pose; lotus; heron pose; pyramid pose. I prefer
rivers: their crooked shores, their lonesome rocks; sand, smooth
as a blood moon.

Dream Song 228

Sometimes there are no dreams. They are replaced with sounds;
sound visions. More often they're quiet: the low shuffle of grass
in a summer breeze; the rumble of wings [always black] against

a humid sky; a voice [background singer] a cappella. I'm too young
to remember stories with happy endings; the street where I grew up
is long gone; the dirty white house at the end of the block, painted

melancholy green. The window I cracked open to sneak a smoke
is boarded up; I would take you there but I'm too afraid you might
be disappointed with the silence.

Dream Song 228

It was the softest part of summer; a day to sandlot away; a day
to fly. I knew the names of all the states in alphabetical order

[capitals too]. She had a pale complexion; homemade dress;
a spot of freckles on her left shoulder blade; and those eyes,

those eyes. I liberated some longnecks; took her to the tracks;
we kicked off our shoes then put our ears to the rail; felt a rumble

as our fingers touched. *I know you by heart* is what she said;
what she really meant was you are not the one not the one.

Dream Song 229

The past is a line in the sand; a naked bulb swinging in an empty
hall; the taste of your skin when it rains. Sometimes, I pretend

to be asleep, eyes closed; the scratch of time cold on my chest.
I hear the low whine of a train approaching; the stifled breath

of desire; your hand touches mine. I am cloud-sopped, heaven-
proof. I will love you when the world is not paying attention;

when it turns its eye to the flight of a bird; its ear to the sound
of a branch as it snaps in this February wind.

Dream Song 32

This is the song of Old Crow; wingless
and forgotten, afraid of a straw sun;
angry with a non-existent god

over forgotten slights.
There are fields and rain, telephone wires;
beaks that scratch the sky's underbelly.

There is love found, love lost;
small suggestions, slight hints of salaciousness.
The fable goes: Crow was snow white,

almost pure. He blackened himself,
sailed into clouds; the warm touch of wind
on his feathers. [he called this,

the dreamed of places]. When he tired of himself,
he created heaven, perched at the right hand of god;
turned the sky deep, shiny and black.

Dream Song 35

We are here, instead of desire; in the country raking leaves
on the forest floor, hair a tangle; a scratch, the length of a thigh

from a raspberry bush; it is a wanting, waiting for the first shoe
to drop. We are crumbs left strewn like flowers for a child bride;

we are fireworks bursting into clouds. It has been years since
you've been gone only moments since you woke. We are here:

do you love me still, do you think of me when the sun shutters
its eyes, when the day goes dark; when we are no longer there.

Dream Song 35

Train Schedule: Platform 6; leaves at 5:15; 3 ½ hours; direct
[I'll press your name to the roof of my mouth]. What did you

want me for; I am a crow with nowhere left to fly. Platform 9;
5 ¾ hours; four stops [Before you, it was all the stories with foggy

endings] Where was the last place we made love; could you find
it again or has it wandered into your imagination. Platform 12;

3 hours; express [the smell of creosote and the sound of wood
snapping in a fire]. Let's lie together at the bottom of the sky.

Dream Song 36

*I would like to be that unnoticed
and that necessary*; read that in a poem;
about variations of sleep;

[someone's idea of love] or maybe she
[Margaret Atwood]
meant something else entirely.

If I met her I would ask: who
was it written for; was it unrequited love,
unfulfilled, desire. I would offer to buy her

a drink [because that's what I do] ask if she
would recite it to me; close my eyes,
imagine it is only us.

[In my mind] she reads past sincerity and into
my metaphor. I am unnoticed, necessary;
one short flight away from epiphany.

Dream Song 312

I rely on words from the dead, waste my breath on a mirage;
walk to the falls, wait for the sun to mist. I'm drawn to water;
a common fetish of a melancholy man. Someone plays violin

[Brahms, Schoenberg?] keeps a cat on a leash. This isn't me
under this bridge [it's my good side] wishing on a ghost, hot
cup of coffee [black] and a last chance. I am mechanical, thin;

birds circle, a dog barks and there I am [again]: in a king bed,
blinds drawn, an unexpected rain; the wet shell of another day
blows to pieces.

Dream Song 315

Dylan [Bob not Thomas] goes on about barbed wire/
hail and hound dogs; I rely on words from the dead

[again and again]. Trees rehearse for spring; shadows
from a V of birds mows across the park. Venus masquerades

as a star; from here we can easily chart a course to surrender.
Dylan [Thomas not Bob] died drunk in St Vincent's;

bones gone, they're swaggering through a winding sea.
You tell me: the thought of words stripped bare makes

your pussy wet; the thought of one fat chance to believe
makes you want to tie me down, fuck me goodbye.

Dream Song 319

You like to say the wind has special powers; to help us
remember, to make us forget. [I fucked a waitress once,

on her break]. You write evasions and koans, call them
haiku: no/still no/good. Outside my window the skyline

slants; grey meets grey meets red blends into a leaf-less
tree [I once practiced suicide with an unloaded gun]. Your

bare feet are immune to gravel, your face sun-reddened,
dress wet; [I remember the first and last time I was drunk]

fall asleep with the light on. I will dream of songs
with no words; a funeral procession through cornfields.

Dream Song 319

Memories: watching the moon die; the sharp twist of a bottle cap,
shredding the inside of my finger. Colors: blue of impatience,

a fragile white [her dress on the day she left], the peeled orange
of the stars [a pretty dream she told me about, the one that didn't

include me]. Lost: torn back pocket, a one off fuck in a deserted
house. Found: the buckle and snap as the sky unfolds; the crash

of dishes off a mantle; the stutter of a lawn mower running out of
gas [Summer 1991]. Solid: rivers that unravel into a surly wind.

Dream Song 319

It starts with want; it always starts with want: [Mary with her small
tits, fast mouth] slow, smooth, a silk stocking [Robin, round assed

and bra-less]; the sweat beading off a beer glass[Lori in her two piece].
There used to be alley's behind our houses; thin routes used to sneak

behind enemy lines, stashed porn and half empty bottles of Paul
Masson. [one taste, then a touch and then another brush with need].

It ends when the room shuts down; a cough and gag of a last smoke;
trying too hard to swallow all a June night has on offer.

Dream Song 321

I miss dial tones, the last echo of voice as the line hums. I miss
the tactile sensation of maps; creases and folds that mark our
progress [our regression], where we have been [where we wish

to go]. If you were French I would kiss your neck, feel the tumble
of leaves, watch as they flutter to the ground [you are freckled].
If you were German I would run my palm over your calf; watch

you Dietrich your way down Kurfurstendamm. [you are a day
that stirs]. Listen: the steady ring of a telephone [anticipation];
we're back on dry land.

Dream Song 321

Out of the country this year on your birthday;
last year, miscommunication
[drunk]; year before,

emergency
at work [fucking another woman];
year before, plain

forgot. Poor excuses poured from
a poor [meaning inadequate;
not pitiable] man.

Four years ago
there was snow on the ground
[Paula was so stoned

she thought you died on your birthday];
today the world breaks into grays
and reds,

a Velvet Underground
day [you wouldn't call it that].
BTW,

going to Paris
[her name is Julia]
you would like her,

call her honey,
ask her to marry you;
ask her if I was still thirsty.

Dream Song 322 [for Julia on her birthday]

I dream Klimt; nightmares are Picasso.
First time I fucked;
Modigliani

[it was summer,
she was in love; I was indifferent].
Drunk is Bernini;

college road trip out west, Monet
[her name was Sarah].
This morning; Cezanne: the tap, tap of rain,

the grunt of a garbage truck in the alley.
I imagine you asleep
[Degas]

the rhythm of your breath
[first time we met; Goya],
color of your hair; Renoir.

Soon, you will wake up, write
[the curve of your neck; Rodin]
of a sleeping field of green,

oceans, mountains;
the taste of loss [Gauguin,
Caravaggio, Hopper and Pollock].

Dream Song 323

It is spring; first we'll find a nice quiet spot in the woods
[no, let's back up a few steps] there should be candles.
Not the long tapered kind or tea light; not scented either

but clean, maybe blood red [you tell me how you like
the feel of wax against your skin]. There will be ribbon,
also red; I could wash your hair [we would create a ritual]

you would lay out my clothes, make coffee. We'll search
for a clearing, midday [or better, late afternoon], a murmur
of rain; the physics of silence folds the sky in two.

Dream Song 323

I will write her a letter; fold it into a map, an antidote to loss.
If it is good enough it will capture the sound of birds in flight,

the smell of fresh cut wood. My youth was misspent on bare
floors and gravel roads. She was nineteen; fiancé in Rochester,

sneaked her mom's smokes, wore glasses; was pretty in an
un-pretty kind of way. I was a crow with tattooed wings, sitting

tight in a high back chair on the wire between sober and drunk;
it was wrong, all wrong all the time; right up to the very end.

Dream Song 326

Still life hangs in the hallway: ashtray, chair, table, empty
bowl [in the name of the father and the son and the holy
ghost]. My un-opened letters bound by string, in a basket;

I remember her favorite dress; pale blue, [I used to hold
her hand] one button gone. I miss the smell of coffee,
the jangle of car keys, the quiet way her voice tightened

when she was nervous; [in the city we die fast, out here
it's so slow]. My fitted shirt is wrinkled, we need rain;
first time in years the river has crested but not flooded.

Dream Song 326

I want to stay true north, follow your footsteps; drive
to the sea, to the horizon; unzip the blue from the sky,

walk in the sand. Navigate using the slopes of barns,
faded red angles drooping under a March sun; turn

the radio all the way down, listen for the small sound
of your voice; an echo in the asphalt. Doing seventy,

I feel the weight of grey tug at the wheels, watch
thin mile markers scarecrow the path to a city buried

on a hill. Its streets and bridges pocked with gravel,
loss; broken pieces from a fallen moon.

Dream Song 327 [Lent]

We're told to give up some luxury; it is penitential, a pious
custom to winnow our sins. Take them away: the black birds

peering at us from a wire [the sin of beauty]; a naked bulb
swinging in the hall [the sin of desire]; a rosewater scent,

the weight of your hand on my arm [the sin of love]; a smudge
of oil on the back of your wrist [the sin of art]. What remains

has nothing to do with our souls; nothing to do with how deep
winter cuts or how abandon can burst a summer sun in two.

Dream Song 327

It wasn't a real tornado but that's what we called it;
shingles ripped from the roof, a crack of electricity

killed the power, scared the kids huddled in the cellar
next to crates of potato wine. There are no answers

in a tempest. Another do-over: the shape your hand
makes in mine; a patch of grass that marks our first

kiss. The eastern part of town is legend; the west
with its churches, bars and rusted tracks. We're torn

and frayed; you had an AM radio with a tinny speaker,
two stations; love songs all sound the same in stereo.

Dream Song 329

It's a silent movie, a sympathy fuck, a note taped to the fridge;
the late night bark of a dog that wants to be let out. It's the to

and fro of an R & B song, the back and forth of a one-sided
conversation; independence from prime numbers and gravity.

There was the slow motion of uncertainty, sawdust and pool
chalk; dense clouds of smoke, hiked up skirts. It's now; it's this

piece of earth clenched in my fist. There was last call, last call,
and final chances; the soft amber glow of a first crush. It is now.

Dream Song 330

We were sinless and uninterrupted [me, high hat handed; feathered
and full], you, shiny; looking all dynamite wrapped in a summer
coat in the middle of February, you kissed me kissed me but never

said goodbye. I sit; testified and hungry, watch every [one] thing
fall: the wasted and the wan, the soundless and thin, the deserved
and the unearthed; the fortunate, unready and unfiltered: ashes,

ashes [we're all fucked up]. The sky is ordinary; we are untogether
and wanting. Your window faces east, I remember paper butterflies
[blue, green, red] on a string; mine is blank and frosted; directionless.

Dream Song 330

We hunted for quiet; legs pumping
hard up hills, bike tires worn bald.

She brought tarot cards,
said her mother was a gypsy;

her voice became small, I tried
to steal a kiss in the dark.

It's been days without rain, the still waters
of Superior drowns the wind.

The air is tight; you always know
what to say;

you have written me a map,
I smell burning wood; the ash.

My future lies bare, I'm at a loss; a fall
leaf blown from sidewalk to street,

the lake hums; you press my name
to the roof of your mouth.

Dream Song 43

I recognize you everywhere: you are a little

bird, your bright wings, a melancholy quiver

that wakes the sky from a deep cloud sleep.

We walk to the river, after the flood; count

star trains. I play with the buttons on your coat.

You bite my lip, speak of moonlit crows, white

hot vigils; mourning and hymns. I tell you stories:

my first car, bench seat and wing windows; a girl

without a name, hiked skirt, black heels; a shared

flask of schnapps. I climb to the top of the hill over

looking the water; throw stones at the devil.

Dream Song 43

Her hands folded, as if in prayer; a neon shadow crosses

the bed, we're a blur of drink and smoke and promises.

It's a safe bet the river will flood soon; the bars will

empty and the all night girls will pretend to run from

the all night boys; someone gets lucky someone gets

lonely; someone always pays. I will not fuck us over,

won't recreate heaven and earth. You are a confession,

a sacrament, keeper of faith; hands clasped as if in prayer.

Tonight the sky holds salvation. The difference between

what's lost and what's holy no longer matters.

Dream Song 44

It was the first day of spring; like any other day but flatter;

a tight-chested-wait-for-the-shoe-to-drop day. We tried to

be good, tried to placate the part time gods. Parked cars

heat up on Main Street. She's newly minted in her halter

top, sling backs and black tights; that buzz should be over

by now. I watch the sun fight shadows on the downtown

skyline; can't keep anything, can't imagine words anymore

without you in them. You play piano: soft, low; a prayer,

a processional song for saints and the forgotten. I have

to say everything twice; make sure I believe.

Dream Song 45

That night I got arrested was star-spangled and dry; a blood

moon wrapped in white gauze. She had my coat. She had

to walk home. It was the last time I made her cry; she loved

me. We are armed and unmanned; too shy to have a childhood

worth remembering. That great lake swallowed us whole;

drowned our handsome voice. Our past lies in a city in a far

off land across an ocean buried in a hill. You're in Chicago;

New York; you're a winter's kiss. We're a made-up dialogue

on the curb; a secret waiting to be shared.

Dream Song 45

We were immortal and invisible; under influenced and loaded.

We surfed the rain on Superior Street; broke bottles and jumped

fences. We became whip-smart and motored up. She saw me

from a high windowed palace. She was a distracted miracle,

a ripened star; another one more chance. That summer is distant,

obscure; we climbed stones and buried sins. You put my hand

on your heart to keep it warm. The sky is a wheat field, fertile

and rich; we are home. In the scent of lilies, the crunch of leaves

we become an element that lives between water and fire.

Dream Song 46

We sat on the ledge at the overlook [Skyline Boulevard];

crushed cans of Special X and Budweiser, contemplated

lengths of rope [right there; a flock of swans taking flight].

She told me she was a hand-me-down, she'd confess to

anyone's sins; [a black V swings over the bridge heading

north]; at midnight in the middle of summer she became

the way the truth the light of my life [the V is a thin line,

a speck]. You tell me longing is a tree, rooted and heaven

-bound; say everything can be measured: sadness, silence;

the distance between loss and redemption.

Dream Song 46

We were kaleidoscopes: splinters of glass and sand;

[she said she knew me]. Turned to the light we bled

into circles and squares; [moved her foot up my leg].

Rough grains slipping round a cylinder [it wasn't even

close to last call]. We woke to the barely dawn, to

the barest of blues and naked pinks; became walking

talking shadows. You're on your way away from me

[your side of the bed; still warm]. Your dress lies

guilty on the floor; a dog-eared paperback [marked

at a poem about Hopper]. Tonight bleeds all colors,

we're alone, together; weightless and unwanting.

Dream Song 49

She was a suicide note, a quiet implausibility
in bed with me. For a moment I forgot her

name. Taking my hand, she told me stories.
Stories to recite in a bar, stories that tasted

of earth; wet and harrowed; I wanted to touch
every syllable, devour them. At the train station,

a kiss good bye. Last words: you tell me to call
you. I rub my hands together to stay warm.

True stories are broken: they've no beginnings,
their middles stretch flat over time.

The endings are uneven; some supple, full;
others cut your bones to a sharp point.

Dream Song 49 [I wait for the day when you tell me to stop writing poems for you]

For you to tell me you have had enough words
and vowels, rivers and flights;
enough consonants

and crows and colors; light and dark.
You've had your fill of the earth and the heavens,
the oceans; roiling seas and vast lakes;

that you no longer need to glimpse the landscape
with its rocks and fog, gulls
and fields; its hills and caves and wildflowers.

Until then, I will tell you how it feels
like rain, how the air tastes of ginger
and cinnamon.

How we are two of a kind; how we will stay
undone, stay bare; unfinished
and unalone.

Dream Song 416

There is nothing but divides; [real and imagined];
all contained in a whorl of dust:
scarred Louisville slugger

leaning in the corner; a girl hiding, afraid
of man-eating bears; an inky reflection
of white [stars]

on glass. We wait at the end of a long line
of pretenders wanting to believe
[craving to believe].

I touch the slight part of your lips,
watch the light play on your jaw;
trace the bone

with the palm of my hand.
There's the sun. It's snowing
in April;

let's fill our mouths, confess
imagined sins; imagined sins
as lovely as the real ones.

Dream Song 417

She told me one day I'd forget how to love

her. The same way a kid forgets how to play

cops and robbers; it's gradual, until one day

the realization hits: it doesn't matter who's

good or bad. It was a wooden bridge; shook

to hell whenever a train passed over. She'd

squeeze my hand, eyes shut tight and wait.

We are windblown; orphans; you tell me

I've made a habit of losing you; that you've

experienced too much loss already. I listen

for the whistle; point my finger at the track,

cock my thumb; *bang bang* you're dead.

Dream Song 418 [...and it burns, burns, burns]

Going to Oz [the land down
under] in a couple days.
I don't like to fly.

It's not the fear of flying
or the fear of crashing
or sudden jolts of turbulence.

I prefer trains; land travel,
the sway and clack of a train
as it bullets through the country.

The smooth hum of an automobile;
windows cranked down, stereo
cranked up; nothing but the swoop

and swirl of crows and hawks
for an escort. Counting mile
markers, you change the station,

look for Johnny Cash. We're going
straight to the end of the world;
going to start a fire.

Dream Song 418

We read all dads' old comics. He had stacks of them.
They were a great way to get through drives to Chicago

or the UP. I read Archie; always knew he should pick
Betty. Somehow she seemed more sincere than Veronica.

You tell me how you used to get carsick; yellow birds
that flit in the ditch; daisies; the patient rhythm of your

mother's breath; how her freckles glistened. The highway
says everything we cannot. Your shoulder is bare;

the perfect place to rest my head. We are true. We are
windblown. We are exactly what we prefer to be.

Dream Song 58

I want to sleep. I do not want to sleep.
Walking on the edge of a building
on the verge of collapse. I cannot
remember. I do not want to remember.

I want to remember
[desperately]
the shape: of her mouth; a grain of sand.

Then: bang bang;
a stream of music from a hole in the sky:
[Lou Reed, Vicious; Sugar, Helpless; Blur, Tender]

I cannot see beauty.
I see beauty.
I cannot remember beauty.

The ocean is dismal;
birds form wicked rain in the forest
[my hand reaches].
Say you will love me. Say you cannot love me.

Dream Song 510

Her father had a car that looked like an Egyptian cat:
stone black; pointed ears, slanted eyes. First time we

kissed she said I reminded her of a beautiful mistake.
I told her I was too honest to tell the truth; stuttered

and stammered my way to third base. Spent the whole
summer trying to escape the city; wore her smile like

a flag. Last night I dreamed you were in a foreign
country, living off air and the tang from the last

time we made love. That's how I wish to remember
you: all light and pale blues; endless.

Dream Song 514

Paint me the sky. I want to remember;

want to remember the fable of the bees.

You told it to me the weekend we lived

with the monks; told me we had to make

love quietly but it was ferocious; as if it

were our last time on earth. When we over-

heard the woman next door praying rosary,

we stifled laughs, hands over mouths;

comfortable in our sin. Then you pinned

my arms to the bed, kissed me hard;

whispered the story. Please. Paint it.

I want to feel the blood buzz; the flutter

of your dress in summer.

Dream Song 518

You said I didn't need permission to love you.

The words didn't matter.

What mattered were skin, breath, and fingers tip to tip.

The place didn't matter.

A home emptied of children.

A house emptied of husbands or wives.

Still attic air.

One window open.

Anyplace where twigs and stems could have their next spring.

It was raining the day we went to the Prado.

It was a day that felt angular, pointed.

I lost you to Velázquez and Goya.

Picasso's *Guernica* was much larger than expected.

Tourists took snapshots.

Lights flashed and bounced.

You and I belonged to abandon.

Dream Song 522 [Self-portrait with regret]

We walk against a surly wind.

You say it's impossible for wind to be surly.

My hands stuffed in too small gloves; my fingers buckle.

You tell me to reconsider buckle.

Let me think a moment.

I'll strip away any pretense.

I want to fuck.

Make it a good, righteous fuck.

Like a second language.

Please.

Be my partner in crime.

Let's fuck our way into art.

Also, you should know:

You are the sea.

You are vast, open; a sanctuary.

I cannot imagine night without your body.

I want to kiss you until there is nothing left but ash.

Dream Song [Self- portrait moments before car crash]

The Rolling Stones are blasting.

Jumping Jack Flash.

I wonder about the sound of metal crunching.

Is it anything like thunder.

Wonder why the line in the middle of the road isn't quite straight.

But it's alright.

Imagine my ex-girlfriend in her favorite dress.

It showed off the perfect amount of leg.

I squeeze my thighs around a half full bottle of beer, turn a hard right.

Or maybe it's wrong.

There's no blinding white light.

No cinematic rewind of my life.

There's black.

The moon is unplugged.

You have forgotten.

But it's alright, now.

In fact it's a gas.

Dream Song 523

I had a dream last night we fucked.

It was so goddamn real.

When I woke there was a half second I thought you were next to me.

We're never where we think we'll be.

I know all the things you would never do.

Have you noticed everything sounds different in your sleep?

The wind is an invisible sea.

A shadow mixed with light is the snap of a wood fire.

Even silence has its own voice.

It's the muffled crack of a bat.

I'm broken.

Bought and paid for.

You are weightless; a birdsong.

I usually don't remember dreams.

Dream Song 523

There's a mallard and his mate, outside my window. The rose bushes have been uprooted; ready to be replaced. Across the street the police are in the process of arresting a woman. Her husband [boyfriend] leans against the building like he's seen it all before. It's difficult. I think I'm ruined. I'll take my chances in slivers; not brave enough to flat out ask and too smart [afraid] to blow it all by being honest. If you were here I couldn't fake it. But you're not. You are a handwritten letter; an untold story. Tomorrow, the landscapers will be back.

Dream Song 523

Now, there is nothing but dirt. They took the trees, bushes; even part of the sidewalk. The police are gone. The flashing red and blue a quiet promise of their return. I want to tell you stories. I want to find one more way to turn the truth. I want to be subversive. I'll confess my crimes. I'll take my chances; tell you what you think you already know. I do plan to post this bundle of letters. Maybe I'll redact them. As if they were sent from a warzone or some Eastern Bloc country; before the wall came down.

Dream Song 524

Sometimes I no longer believe you are real; this letter
will sit in the dead letter office. Unopened and unread
until one rainy day, a bored employee will wonder who
it was meant for. They will open it, read it aloud; create
their own narrative. I wonder will they be able to see
the curve of your hand, the spot on your wrist I used
to kiss; the freckle on your rib. On my window ledge,
a petal, used to be a rose. It is a stamp that has fallen
off an envelope; one more letter unable to be delivered.

Dream Song 525

I think about carefully writing letters
then leaving them in random places:

Dear Subway Passenger,
Dear Passer-By,

Let me tell you about my lover. She's beautiful in that way
sadness has of rounding out edges. She likes to go barefoot;
better to feel the earth tremble, she says. She worries about
the sun when it rains. Likes to sit in her grandmother's chair;
best seat in the house when it thunders. She believes in long
good-byes and wide-open spaces. Last thing she told me was
how words seem to come alive, when written by hand.

Dream Song 529 [Aqua City]

It was a familiar place but brand new. It was warm, not spring but not quite the full of summer. We'd been traveling. I remember the feeling of road dust, weariness but the kind that is restful. We were in bed; fully clothed. You told me stories. Black and white tales of your parents; when you were a little girl, skinned knees, a red princess bike. How you were afraid of winter. Your head cradled in my shoulder your voice got softer, lower as if you were falling asleep. But we were wide awake. Wide awake the whole time.

Dream Song 529

Every day I stop at the park. Same time, except on Thursdays
[I'm a little late]. I lean against the car and wait. Sometimes
I'll walk the path. Once I sat under a maple; watched a robin
collect twigs for a nest. One day there will be nothing left to
breathe; a few moments here, a question or two there. I notice
the same people: an older woman sits on the bench facing west
[always leaves at 4:30], a young boy and girl, [the beginnings
of a crush]. Sometimes, I wonder if they recognize me; know
what I'm waiting for.

Dream Song 530

I tell you about my first: 50/50 tickets wrapped around her waist; gave her $5.00. She lifted her dress, kissed me good luck, slid a number in my hand. A promise made in the comfort of a moment. You and I become thirsty. There is a prayer in my pocket in the event of an emergency; there's a wingspan beneath us. You say I am a thief of fire; hold the ashes to prove it. Tell me you like to make me smile; laugh, call it your job. We are two branches. We sway; moonlight wet on our bare feet.

Dream Song 531

You tell me nine is your favorite number; its constancy,
its simplicity and solitude; fragility filled with resilience.
It's a cloud pilfered from the sky, a bare wind; detritus
the birds use to build a nest. It's a nursery rhyme sung
by a child, the familiar clamor of dinner dishes in the sink.
It is a tree that stands alone in a yellow field, a postscript
to a letter. It's rain that appears from nowhere; a stopped
clock, laughter in a quiet theater. It's the last stop for gas
on 35W before you're here; it's a way to always remember.

Dream Song 66

I love edges. Anything that can take me down another city
block, around corners; into the permanent. The air is lousy
with shouts from irritated cars. It's all breakable; you tell
me joy is the number 8, always doubling back on itself.
There is a catch in your voice; you would rather be home,
digging in the garden until the sensation of floating ebbs
into a drop of rain. I want to plan a full color escape, feel
the brush of your hand against my cheek. Until everything
is simple math: minus me; plus you; divide us both in two.

Dream Song 67

Remember the night we stole your father's car? The halo-glow
of the porch light illuminated our crime. You slid across the long
bench seat, told me to drive. Drive to nowhere; drive over the edge
of the earth; watch the look on God's face as we crack the horizon.
I remember crickets singing louder the further we went; the hum
of wind through wing windows. There was clean static from AM
radio; your hand on mine. I wake, three four five times a night
and you're invisible; a shadow; a heart-shaped moth watching
over me as I fall to sleep.

Dream Song 611

Not sure what is left to write. I've told you about the birds that nest
in winter; the simple pearl of water that glides down my window;
an unpainted bridge over Lester Park Creek that reminds me of that
summer. We cannot forget what we don't remember; cannot let it
go again. Next time will be forever. This morning the moon was a dim
light wrapped in gauze. We are separated; not by distance, not time
but circumstance. We will carry each other; two butterflies frozen still
on pink petals. Handwritten notes folded in our pockets; everything
we'll ever need.

Dream Song 612

I want you to forget you love me. Forget how trees scallop the sky,
the way the horizon shuns the stars. I want you to bury the words
you gave to me. The ones that belong to the soft rush of wind
through pussy willows. Pack away the quiet adjectives you use
to describe the sound of morning; forget it all. I'll write you from
another continent, bare and thirsty words; underfed and worthless
words. I'll write of broken promises; made up prayers from lost
lovers. I'll tell you about paper wings, ashes; a wet moon awash
on the shore.

Dream Song 614

I'm looking outside my window 5:30AM; the only
one here; not ready to work. Its quiet; the quiet
roar of a world that's still and within itself. You tell
me you are flying out in five days; England then
Portugal. I wonder what love feels like after a distance;
after silence turns into a rush of wind. Later this year
I'll be in London; funny how we end up in the same
places but never at the same time. Send me a card,
a cheap souvenir. I'll fold it into a talisman; every
crease a reminder of where I've been.

Dream Song 615 [I still think of you when the world gets like this]

How you told me 11 is the number for clarity;
it's morning, rivers and sleet. It's anything
wet: sweat on a glass of beer, a splash from
fish, silver and sleek. It comes before blood,
before we learn how to swallow loss. You love
this town, its broken pieces laid out before this
Great Lake. The park by the canal is deserted,
gulls pick at tourist leftovers. I imagine you
painting, writing, listening to your favorite
playlist; *firefly* or *lush*. I watch the lights on
the hill go out one by one by one; count them
until everything becomes clear.

Dream Song 618

I want to lie with you on a narrow bed
in a simple room; a plain white sheet,
blank walls. There's one window; outside
a field, then woods. Your arms wrapped
lightly around me. Your blouse, sweater
and green skirt with the frayed hem hang
over the back of a rocking chair; bra and
panties on the floor at the foot of the bed.
There's a bell, a quiet chime; it's Sunday
morning. The slant of rain is illuminated
by the moon. We're unafraid, marooned
as long as we choose; lost on this blue
quilted sea between dreams and sleep.

Dream Song 619

By now, you're over the ocean; there's the rustle
of pages being turned, the flicker of dim lights.
The scent of the moon has followed you, clings
to your skin. Before you close your eyes, I will
tell you this: there's nothing the air cannot hold;
the soft crescendo of leaves in winter, the splash
of a fish in summer, a grass-stained knee; even
this letter folded in your pocket. I'll find your
favorite tree. Take a twig, soft brown and brittle,
put it on the window ledge; wait for a bird to pick
it up, fly it to you.

Dream Song 621

I remember things not related to love: how one day
you took off your wedding band to see if he would
notice; how Francis is your favorite saint; how the
color orange tastes like grief. The days are starting
to get shorter; wish I was someplace deep and green.
Do you know I love your imperfections? Each one is
the perfect sin. There's a moving van across the street;
a plane unzips the blue from the sky. The downtown
skyline is a layer of gray. The landscaping is all done;
the mallard and his mate have been gone for days.

Dream Song 622

What will be left after you have truly gone: a frayed end of thread from your sweater; a bare bulb flickering in the closet; a dog-eared book with a coffee stained cover? There is no past. I'll pick now to remember what it was like; the scent of rosewater and wood smoke, the rumble of wings against sky as I watch you tie back your hair. There is no such thing as forgiveness or second chances. I'd rather drink to sin; picture you at the end of the bar, hair shorn, legs crossed high ready to start a revolution.

Dream Song 628

She was from Key West; I liked the way it sounded
bohemian and Hemingway; shotguns and giant marlin.
It suited her mood: heavy, humid, like swimming through
a perspiring sun. Before this flood she worked as a waitress.
Cool Joe tended bar. It was all H-Bomb martinis, tits & legs
& whispering palms. She never trusted him, his too sharp
switchblade smile; she had a plan, bulletproof and straight.
We're a generation of cunts he'd say, twisting another
lemon rind round another rim. She heard the crack of ice,
felt the rush of rivers, the cold snap of February's wind.

Dream Song 628

She's shambolic; a calculated wreck, all legs and long hair
waiting for the bottom to drop out and the top to level off.
It's the end of the line. Light is muffled and not a goddamn
cop in sight when you really need one. But we're not afraid
of trouble. There is closing time, after party burnout time,
love, hate and muscle; over played hands and underhanded
plays. We're rolling thunder. We're the chosen ones, baptized
in the wet dew of morning. She meditates on a tear in her
stocking; I feel the cool burn of metal against my forehead.

Dream Song 75

We talk about ghosts while the moon possums in the sky.
It is still; the kind of stillness right before a thunderstorm
or a car crash. We're sitting on the swings; the playground
overlooks the baseball diamond. Colored paper and matches
confetti the infield; shreds from spent bottle-rockets and fire
crackers. Longneck Budweiser's mark first second third base
and home. The only light left is a lone firefly. You've dyed
your hair; skin, white as cuttlefish bones. Tell me your first
wish was the smoothest stone ever skipped across water;
how you felt yourself drown in each ripple and wave.

Dream Song 76

Open the door. It's a balcony room;
its solid sea top to bottom, I never know
when you'll show up.

Wildwood dreams and parked cars;
somewhere a bird, what kind I can't tell
but you're in a hurry.

Don't wait; now, the coffee's boiled over.
You have a husband, children
and a dog; the buzz of a room service bell.

Here's the [our] last leg.
The television is blurred; Jai Alai on sound off.
Two dollar bets and torn tickets.

We're mobile.
We're Crown Vic'ed and convertible.
I love you.

I love you. Don't forget
your wrap.
It's getting cold.

Dream Song 76

Two cars in the lot; one, hood up and doors sprawled open;
the other shy in its expensiveness, trying to hide. No screens
on the lowest rent rooms. It's extra for AC; there's a plastic
cup on the mantle of an unused fireplace. Our flesh shines
from rain and sweat and misunderstanding; one thin bath
towel to share. I help to take off your grandmother's necklace;
every strand a link, a reminder of names you've given yourself:
lonely and *forgotten* and *forlorn*. Outside the heat index hits
105; we'll trade our skin for water; inch by inch let go.

Dream Song 79

We've become the space between words; the period that separates thoughts. This is how we make love now: silent and parenthetically; nothing but the echo of skin against skin. We're fragments of color, black & white scraps of sentence; left to the mercy of unsigned letters, misdialed phone calls and e-mail. At the park on 27th, I lean against my car, wait for the clouds to blush. You'll become rain; I'll become the birdsong. I remember you told me how water will save us; our limbs will dissolve into small waves; how we'll tumble and roll onto a familiar shore.

Dream Song 710

Your favorite things: Sleater-Kinney, driving the freeway
before dawn, Cloud Cult, making a fist, Radiohead, rolling
your pant legs up. The day we met you were going to Nye's
Polonaise; wrote directions on a napkin, called it a poem.
Later, you introduce the guy on your arm as a bass player
in some local band. He references the ending of Great Gatsby
half a dozen times; calls me Nick Carraway. You spill your drink,
say you will write a story after me; recite it in the bar. I count
100 back to zero, start over; pretend we had a chance.

Dream Song 712

We were American lo-fi, civil and disobedient. We were brave.
The sky was fallow. She'd been gone for weeks. We sat in her car
on St Anthony Main; before everything became gentrified. Moments
later she suggested we go to her place. On the sofa, her dog licked
my face. She laughed, unbuttoned my pants. It was fall; no, spring.
No, I can't remember. Afterwards, we didn't shower. She wanted
to keep the scent of my skin. She was impatient; no, maybe sad.
I really don't remember. Maybe I wasn't there. Maybe it's a story
she tells to keep me away.

Dream Song 716

I remember making you cry; remember the first gift you gave me,
a book of stories about lovers and cities. I remember giving you
away, remember the first postcard; wanderlust, Johnny Cash
and open skies. I remember the first time we made love; frantic,
hungry. I no longer dream; am content with blanks, empty space.
That last time, where did you say you were? Was it some dry land
waiting for the sea; in some foreign country piecing the language
together? Here, the sky remains the same. The clouds, the birds,
the dirt, the grass; the reminders, all the same.

Dream Song 718

I've always been a coward; have always excelled at parlor tricks.
That first day, our fingers barely touched, you brushed your hair
aside as you smiled. That last day, the one that proved one can

never plan an ending, I threw my phone out the car window
just past the Riverside exit. Watched in the rear-view as it arced
onto the shoulder, twisting in the air like a Cadillac rolling down

a hill. Somehow, I thought your voice might shatter with the plastic
case, become muffled inside the bent SIM card. Look closely; now
you see me; now you don't.

Dream Song 719

Found an iPod in Canal Park on the stone steps to the lighthouse.
The *Sam Laud* was coming in; the Aerial Bridge at half mast, gulls
perched on the rocks. Can't stand this town, how it swallowed you;

could never stomach its destitute air and rough sand. Going blind
at the 'Toga; watching Miss Pepsi, the Valentine Voodoo Rhythms
and what's-her-name. The one that lip synced everything.

Took her home one night; we were half in the bag, fully lusted,
dangerously armed. The big ship passes; taxis honk, cameras snap
and flash; I click on the playlist, *nothing but time*.

Dream Song 720

Paper bags being blown down the street is art; grey tombstones with their faded stories and numbers; [you're bare feet and wine] a flash of neon, broken glass; a 24 hour convenience store; an empty parking lot; [you're milkweed and wind] ice cubes and earth; a deck of cards and killer hangovers. Shadows on the sidewalk are art; that kid who just whooped because he dunked the ball; [you're beach grass and dunes] the ant crawling on top of my monitor right now; an engine revving, the smell of burnt rubber; [you're watercolor and oils] the space between us now.

Dream Song 722 &723

You were un-ghostly and jagged, black La Perla bra
under a wrecked flannel shirt.

It always seemed to be rain or grey or sleet or clouds;
except for the one weekend of silence and tears.

We were jet-lagged and culture shocked; clichéd
and too cold for summer. I still smoked but hadn't stopped

writing yet, liked to kiss the scar behind your ear,
told you we were birdsongs; immortal.

We had gravel driveways, weed and beer and bench seats
and bald tires. We watched the ships come and go, you wanted

to paint them; paint every place they came from. You imagined
tall pines and red roofed barns,

two-story homes with screen doors and porch swings. Told me
you relied on the lake to keep you strong, felt the need to swim;

wash away the guilt. I hear you've a house
in the city; teach kids, read stories in coffee shops,

have become too familiar with loss. I've given up Berryman,
Henry and Mr. Bones. I lied when I tossed that stone in the lake,

called it a wish, lied when I took your hand that time
we made love by the creek; when I said I'd never forget you.

Acknowledgements:

Dream Songs 227, 228, 228, 229, 32, 35, 35, 36, 312, 315, appeared in White Knuckle Press as a Chapbook; Dream Songs

Dream Songs 75, 76, 76, 79, 79 appeared in the Origami Poems Project as a chapbook; A Cabal of Angels

Dream Songs 622, 628, 628, 710, 712 appeared in the Origami Poems Project as a chapbook;
A Cabal of Angels Pt 2

Dream Songs 523, 523, 524, 525, 529 appeared in the Origami Poems Project as a chapbook;
Dead Letter Office